Fun Things
to Do with
Cardboard
Tubes

by Marne Ventura

CAPSTONE PRESS
a capstone imprint

A+ Books are published by Capstone Press,
1710 Roe Crest Drive, North Mankato, Minnesota 56003
www.capstonepub.com

Library of Congress Cataloging-in-Publication Data
Ventura, Marne.
Fun Things to Do with Cardboard Tubes/by Marne Ventura.
pages cm.—(10 Things to Do)
Audience: Age 5–8.
Audience: K to grade 3.
Includes bibliographical references.
Summary: "Full-color photos and simple, step-by-step instructions describe 10 crafts and activities using
cardboard tubes and common materials found around the house"—Provided by publisher.
ISBN 978-1-4765-9895-6 (library binding)
ISBN 978-1-4765-9899-4 (ebook pdf)
1. Cardboard tube craft—Juvenile literature. I. Title.
TT870.V46 2014
745.5—dc23   2014012753

Editorial Credits
Jeni Wittrock, editor; Bobbie Nuytten, designer; Sarah Schuette, photo stylist; Marcy Morin, studio scheduler;
Kim Braun, project production; Tori Abraham, production specialist

Photo Credits
Images by Capstone Studio: Karon Dubke except Shutterstock: Nata-Art, swirl design, Seamartini graphics,
floral design

Printed in the United States of America in
North Mankato, Minnesota
032014   008087CGF14

Table of Contents

Introduction 4

I Spy Binoculars 6

Wild and Woolly 8

Musical Maracas 12

Sneaky Snake 14

Perfect Party Favors 16

Nature Wall Hanging 18

Hot Rod Racer 20

Kooky Kazoo 24

Owl Family
Finger Puppets 26

Mighty Microphone 30

Read More 32

Internet Sites 32

Introduction

Uh-oh! You used up the last of the roll of toilet paper. You replaced it with a new roll, but what do you do with the empty tube? Throw it away? Not a chance!

If you like making easy crafts and want to help Earth by recycling, you are in luck. All of the projects in this book start with a cardboard tube found inside a toilet paper roll. Add a few basic tools and materials, and—presto! You have something new!

Are you ready to get started? Try out all these awesome cardboard tube projects. Then think up some new projects of your own!

I Spy Binoculars

Supplies

» 2 cardboard tubes
» silver paper
   or silver paint
» black paper strips
» clear tape
» stapler
» black string

1. Tape silver paper around each tube (or paint with silver paint).

2. Tape the strips of black paper around one end of each tube.

3. Staple the tubes together, side by side.

4. Staple one end of the string to the outside of each silver end.

SCHOOL

Wild and Woolly

Supplies

- » pencil
- » cardboard tube
- » 2 black stir sticks
- » scissors
- » cotton balls
- » white glue
- » black paper or craft foam
- » white paper or craft foam
- » stick-on wiggly eyes

1 With the point of a pencil, poke four holes in the tube for legs. Make the holes small enough so that the stir sticks will fit snugly.

2 Cut the stir sticks in half. Poke half a stir stick into each hole.

3 Stuff cotton balls into each end of the tube.

4 Glue cotton balls all over the tube.

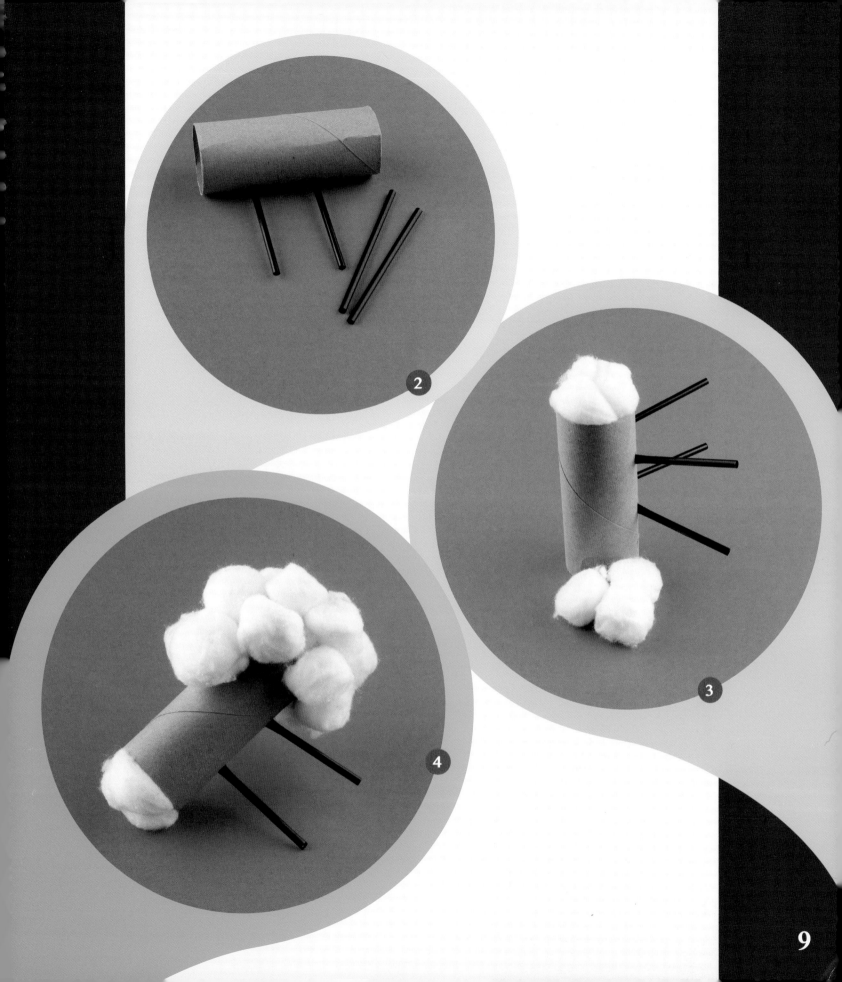

Cut a face with ears from black craft foam. Cut a cloud shape from white craft foam. Stick on the wiggly eyes. Glue on the white foam fur.

6 Glue the face to one end of the tube.

Step It Up: Use pom-poms instead of cotton balls to make a black sheep.

5

6

Musical Maracas

Supplies

» cardboard tube
» 2 waxed paper circles (a cottage cheese or yogurt lid makes a good pattern)
» clear tape
» a handful of small dry beans
» craft paper or construction paper

1 Cover one opening of the tube with waxed paper. Tape it in place.

2 Put the beans inside the tube.

3 Cover the other opening of the tube with waxed paper and tape it in place.

4 Tape craft paper around the tube. Decorate with strips of other colors to make it brighter.

Sneaky Snake

Supplies

» 7 cardboard tubes
» scissors
» acrylic paint
» paintbrush
» 14 brads
» 2 stick-on wiggly eyes
» red construction paper
» clear tape

1 Flatten the tubes gently. Start at the center of each open end and cut a diagonal line to the flattened side so that both ends of the tube are pointed. Do this for each tube.

2 Paint the tubes and let them dry.

3 Use the pointed end of a brad to poke holes in all four points of each tube. For two tubes, only punch holes on one end. These will be the head and the tail.

4 Use brads to attach the tubes, top and bottom. Be sure to put the head and tail tubes on the ends. Now your snake can slither!

5 Stick the snake's eyes on its head.

6 Cut a forked tongue from red construction paper. Tape the tongue inside the head so it sticks out the mouth.

Step It Up: Hide the snake for a friend. Give your friend clues as he looks for it. Say "warm" if he's getting closer and "cool" if he's getting farther away.

Perfect Party Favors

Supplies

- » 1 cardboard tube for each favor
- » a few small wrapped candies or toys for each favor
- » clear tape
- » colored tissue paper
- » scissors
- » curling ribbon
- » glitter or stickers to match your party theme

1 Put a few treats inside a cardboard tube. Cover both ends with tape.

2 Stack four pieces of tissue paper. Wrap them around the tube and tape them in place. If the paper is a lot longer than the tube, trim a little off the ends.

3 Tie each end with ribbon. Ask an adult to curl the ribbon. Cut the ends of the paper into strips to make fringe.

4 Decorate the wrapped favors to match your party theme.

17

Nature Wall Hanging

Supplies

» cardboard tube
» cardstock
» pencil
» scissors
» hole punch
» acrylic paint
» paintbrush
» hole punch
» 18 inches (0.5 meter) of yarn or string
» 12 beads
» small items collected during a nature walk
» white glue

 Cut six circles out of cardstock. Use a cardboard tube as a pattern.

 Gently flatten the cardboard tube so it's easier to cut. Then cut it into three rings. Paint the rings inside and out. Let them dry.

3 Punch a hole in the top and bottom of each ring.

4 String three beads onto the yarn. Add one ring and repeat. Tie the yarn around the bottom bead. Trim off the end. At the other end of the yarn, make a loop so you can hang your project.

5 Inside each ring, glue two circles back-to-back with the yarn between them

 Glue one small nature item to each circle.

Step It Up: Loop your nature wall hanging over a doorknob or on a hook on the wall. It also makes a nice gift for a friend!

Hot Rod Racer

Supplies

» cardboard tube
» scissors
» acrylic paint
» paintbrush
» plastic bottle cap
» black marker
» white glue
» 2 small craft foam circles
» craft paper or construction paper
» 4 black craft foam circles
» 4 brads

 Cut a square in the top of the tube. This will be the driver's seat.

 Paint the tube and let it dry.

 Draw a steering wheel on a plastic bottle cap with a black marker.

 Glue the steering wheel in place in front of the driver's seat.

5 Write the number of your hot rod on the two small craft foam circles. Glue them to the sides.

Step It Up: Use masking tape and markers to make a racetrack on a long sheet of paper. Ready, set, go!

6 Cut three small stripes out of construction paper. Glue two strips on the front end and one on the back.

7 Make wheels out of the larger craft foam circles and construction paper. Push the pointed end of a brad through each wheel.

8 Push the brads through the tube to attach two wheels to both sides.

Kooky Kazoo

Supplies

- » cardboard tube
- » scissors
- » ruler
- » clear tape
- » tissue paper, markers, stickers, or sequins
- » glue
- » hole punch
- » wax-paper circle
- » rubber band

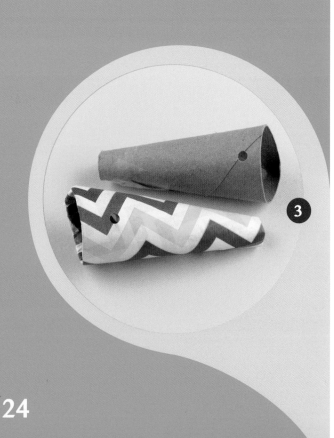

1 Cut a 4-inch (10-cm) slit up the side of a tube. Slide one side of the slit under the other to form a cone. Leave a small opening. Secure with tape.

2 Decorate the tube using markers, tissue paper, sequins, or stickers.

3 Use the hole punch to make a hole near the larger end of the tube, on the side opposite the seam.

4 Use a rubber band to fasten the wax-paper circle to the larger end of the kazoo. Leave the other end open.

Step It Up: To play a crazy kazoo tune, just hum into the open end. Try singing by saying "toot-toot-toot!" The kazoo makes sound because your voice shakes and rattles the wax paper.

Owl Family
Finger Puppets

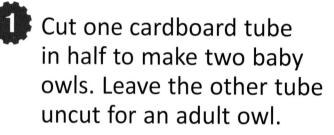

Supplies

- » 2 cardboard tubes
- » acrylic paint
- » paintbrush
- » craft paper or construction paper
- » white glue
- » stick-on wiggly eyes
- » scissors
- » small decorations, such as a tiny bow

 1 Cut one cardboard tube in half to make two baby owls. Leave the other tube uncut for an adult owl.

 2 Flatten all tubes a bit. On one end of each tube, push the edges down in the center to form the owl's pointy ears.

 3 Paint the tubes and let them dry. Make each owl a different color.

 4 Stick two wiggly eyes on each tube.

5 Cut paper triangles for beaks and glue them under the eyes.

6 Cut two paper wings for each owl. Glue them to the owls' sides. Add any decorations you like.

6

Step It Up: With friends, take turns holding an owl puppet on two fingers and ask "Whoo am I?" Give clues—for example: "I was the first president of the United States. Whoo am I?" The first person to guess "George Washington" holds an owl puppet and asks "Whoo am I?" next.

Mighty Microphone

Supplies

» cardboard tube
» black acrylic paint
» paintbrush
» aluminum foil
» paper towel
» black yarn or string
» 2 silver sequins
» white glue

1. Paint the cardboard tube with black paint. Let it dry.

2. Tape a strip of foil around one end of the tube.

3. Scrunch the paper towel into a ball. Lay the ball in the center of a sheet of foil. Wrap the foil around the ball.

4. Press the ends of the foil together like a tail. Tie the end of the string around the tail.

5. Push the tail into the silver end of the tube so the yarn hangs out of the bottom like a cord.

6. Glue the sequins onto the tube for ON/OFF or VOLUME switches.

Step It Up: The mighty microphone transforms its user into a star. Get up on stage and sing a song, tell a joke, or give a speech.

31

Read More

Hardy, Emma. *Green Crafts for Children: 35 Step-by-Step Projects Using Natural, Recycled, and Found Materials*. London, England: CICO Books, 2008.

Speechley, Greta. *Backyard Crafts*. Creative Crafts for Kids. New York: Gareth Stevens, 2010.

Ventura, Marne. *Fun Things to Do with Milk Jugs.* 10 Things to Do. North Mankato, Minn.: Capstone Press, 2015.

Internet Sites

FactHound offers a safe, fun way to find Internet sites related to this book. All of the sites on FactHound have been researched by our staff.

Here's all you do:

Visit *www.facthound.com*

Type in this code: 9781476598956